.

Australian GEOGRAPHIC
explorers

NATIONAL PARKS
OUR WILD HERITAGE

Welcome to

Australian GEOGRAPHIC

explorers

Did you know that Australia has one of the world's best systems of reserves to protect all its different habitats? And just as well, because many of our plants and animals are found nowhere else in the world! This issue will introduce you to some of the 9000 national parks and other protected areas in our National Reserve System that are designed to conserve habitats forever. We'll also help you discover our World Heritage Areas, Indigenous Protected Areas and marine parks. You'll walk down Australia's wildlife corridors, see some endangered plants and animals, and meet a ranger who lives on one of Australia's remote island territories. Enjoy exploring the wild treasures of Australia with us!

– The AUSTRALIAN GEOGRAPHIC team

Contents

4 Our National Reserve System
A quick summary of the range and extent of Australia's parks.

6 Our biggest national park
Kakadu National Park, in the Northern Territory, is a landscape that changes hugely every year.

8 What are wildlife corridors?
Find out the names of the three big connected areas that will help wildlife.

10 Gilbert's potoroo
Meet the rarest marsupial in the world, found in Western Australia.

11 Fantastic flowers
There are more than 1200 species of orchid in Australia, and many of these flowers are endangered.

12 Royal beauty
Royal National Park, found south of Sydney, is the second-oldest national park in the world.

14 Life from the ashes
How do our plants and animals recover after a bushfire?

16 World Heritage
With thousands of listings, the World Heritage List is one of the most important conservation tools in the world.

18 Australia's World Heritage areas
Discover the 19 Australian treasures on the World Heritage List.

20 Tasmania's finest
Walk through gorgeous Cradle Mountain-Lake St Clair National Park.

22 Indigenous Protected Areas
There are 50 of these across Australia, including Australia's largest conservation reserve.

24 Island dingoes
Dealing with a tricky native dog issue on Fraser Island, Queensland.

26 Protecting the seas
Australia is building the world's most extensive marine park system.

28 Let's rock!
At the centre of Australia, Uluṟu-Kata Tjuṯa National Park has some of our most recognised rocks.

30 Meet a ranger
Max Orchard is a ranger on Christmas Island in the Indian Ocean.

32 Glossary
Meanings of some of the trickier words in this issue.

33 Further reading & internet sites
Want more? Go to these websites.

34 Index
A list of what we've covered.

35 Last shot
Beach kangaroo!

3

Fast facts

The largest land-based protected area in Australia is the Tanami Indigenous Protected Area in the Northern Territory, covering 101,500sq.km.

Australia's reserves protect about 10% of the world's plant and animal species.

About 63% of the land in the system is governed by federal, state or territory governments, about 23% by indigenous groups and the rest by private landholders and conservation organisations.

Australia has one of the most extensive conservation estates in the world, including more than 9700 national parks, private land, reserves, World Heritage areas and other protected areas.

Rather than just protecting individual species, the National Reserve System aims to protect a significant sample of every kind of Australian ecosystem, in 89 recognised bioregions.

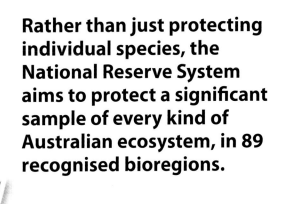

This National Reserve System takes up more than 13% of Australia's land area – more than 1 million square kilometres.

An escarpment, like this on overlooking a Kakadu floodplain at Ubirr, is a long, cliff-like bit of rock.

Kakadu

Keeper of the Northern Territory's natural treasures.

A stunning national park of big contrasts, Kakadu floods in the November–April wet season, when water thunders off the escarpments.

Its vast plains become lush, freshwater wetlands covered in blue-green spear grass. But, by the middle of the year, the park turns to more of a reddy brown colour, its dry woodlands punctuated with termite mounds and shrinking billabongs.

Encompassing 19,804sq.km in the north of the Northern Territory, Kakadu is Australia's largest national park. It takes 2–4 hours to drive there from Darwin.

In terms of animals, Kakadu is best known for the saltwater crocodiles that lurk in the billabongs and waterways, but it also has more than 100 other reptile species, including turtles, snakes and lizards, as well as 280 bird species and 26 types of frog.

Many endangered and vulnerable animals make their homes in Kakadu National Park, including the bare-rumped sheathtail bat, Gouldian finch, olive ridley turtle and the northern river shark.

Aboriginals are estimated to have lived in Kakadu for more than 50,000 years and there are about 15,000 rock-art sites there. Some depict indigenous Australians meeting Macassan, Chinese and European people. Currently about 500 Aboriginal people live in the park.

Rock art, crocodiles, rare Gouldian finches (right) and thundering waterfalls attract visitors to Kakadu.

Billabongs and floodplains help support more than 280 bird and 26 frogs such as the green tree frog (right).

DID YOU KNOW?
The Bininj/Mungguy Aboriginal people of the Kakadu region recognise that there are six seasons, not four. "Wurrgeng" is the season in the middle of the year, when southern Australia is in winter.

Native animals sometimes need to move across large areas of land as their habitats change.

What are wildlife corridors?

In many areas where animals used to moved freely, humans have built towns and industries, or cleared land for farming. In many cases, the animals have been restricted to small areas of remaining habitat, often isolated from other bushland.

Wildlife corridors are connected areas of bushland that allow animals to move more freely in the face of climate change and local disasters, or so they can find a breeding partner. They help make habitat patches bigger and less isolated. Sometimes a farmer will decide not to clear part of their land to help make a corridor between two patches of bush adjoining their land.

The three corridors

Scientists and conservationists are trying to establish three very large wildlife corridors in Australia:

TRANS-AUSTRALIA ECO-LINK

This corridor goes for 3500km through the heart of the country, through savannahs, deserts and forests, from Arnhem Land in the Northern Territory to Port Augusta on the coast of South Australia.

GREAT EASTERN RANGES

This corridor goes 2800km from the Atherton Tableland in Queensland to the Victorian Alps, and is home to more than 8000 species, including the spotted-tailed quoll, swift parrot and squirrel glider.

NORTHERN TERRITORY

WESTERN AUSTRALIA

QUEENSLAND

SOUTH AUSTRALIA

NEW SOUTH WALES

ACT

VICTORIA

TASMANIA

GONDWANA LINK

The Gondwana Link is in south-west Western Australia and joins coastal karri forests to mallee bordering the great Nullarbor Plain. It aims to protect species such as the tiny honey possum, or noolbenger.

Private landowners are providing more habitat by replanting native plants, especially along creek lines.

ILLUSTRATION: ROBERT KAYGANICH

FIGURES
Weight: about 1kg
Head and body length: 27cm
Tail length: 21cm
Food: underground fungi sometimes called truffles

Volunteers (below) record the weight and measurements of a female potoroo (above)

Highly endangered
Gilbert's Potoroo

One of the world's rarest marsupial is a rabbit-sized wallaby-like creature called Gilbert's potoroo. There are estimated to be just 100 of the creatures currently living.

Once thought to be extinct, the species was rediscovered in 1994 at Two Peoples Bay, on the southern coast of Western Australia. In 2005, ten were taken to nearby Bald Island. There they began breeding, free from feral cats and foxes, which kill unsuspecting potoroos.

By 2010, enough had bred on the island to try starting another mainland population in a bush enclosure at Two Peoples Bay, which is protected by an 8.2km fence designed to keep out cats and foxes.

Fabulous flowers

Some orchids pretend to be female wasps.

Many of the most beautiful flowers in the Australian bush are orchids, and there are more than 1200 species in the country. Lots of them are rare and endangered.

As well as being beautiful, they have a few tricks. Some emit a smell like a female wasp. Male wasps are attracted to the flower, thinking they are going to find a female wasp, but instead, end up spreading the orchid's pollen, which helps the orchids create seeds for the next lot of orchids.

Spider orchids (top) mimic female wasps. Below it is a vanilla and scented sun orchid hybrid.

TOP: BILL BACHMAN; BOTTOM: JIRI LOCHMAN

Royal Beauty

Australia is home to world's second oldest national park.

Royal National Park, on the southern side of Sydney, is the second oldest national park in the world, after Yellowstone, in the United States of America. It was first gazetted in 1879 and its 16,000ha include a large variety of habitats: dry, open forests, rainforests, coastal heathland rich in wildflowers, mangroves, freshwater swamps, salt marshes, dramatic coastal cliffs and 10 beaches. Because the Royal has so many different habitats, it is one of Australia's most biologically rich parks, with more than 1000 plant species, and 300 types of bird, including the green catbird, superb lyrebird and large forest owls.

The park is often affected by bushfires, and although many Australian plants benefit from or need fire to reproduce, the fires occur too frequently in some areas for the plants to recover.

More than 2 million people visit Royal National Park each year, among them surfers, anglers, bushwalkers, scuba-divers, cyclists, swimmers, kayakers and picnickers. One of the most popular activities is the 26km two-day hike that runs the length of the park's rugged coastline.

When it was first created as a national park, areas such as Audley were cleared of native vegetation, and picnic areas, gardens, boat facilities and a dance hall were built.

The area is part of the traditional lands of the Dharawal Aboriginal people, and the park protects many of their traditional sites and artefacts. You can see Aboriginal rock carvings at several places, including Jibbon Point, near Bundeena.

iodiverse Royal National Park features a range of habitats, from freshwater rivers to coastal heathland.

CLOCKWISE FROM TOP: ESTER BEATON, GETTY, ESTHER BEATON, GETTY

Darters (above) and eastern water dragons (right) make use of the park's rivers, such as Port Hacking River.

Life from the ashes

Fires often rip through our national parks, but many of Australia's plants and animals have strategies to cope with – or even benefit from – bushfires.

Animals such as the yellow-tailed black-cockatoo and flame robin return to a fire-affected area to feed on insects and regenerating plants.

Some plants such as tree ferns recover quickly from fire, taking advantage of the extra sunlight created by the destruction of the forest canopy. This gives them a head start on other plants.

Trees such as the myrtle beech have a woody swelling called a lignotuber, at soil level or underground, insulated against fire. It's like an emergency storehouse, and when the top of the tree is destroyed, buds inside the lignotuber tap into the root system and burst into new growth.

Seeds, such as those of the mountain hickory wattle, can lie in the soil for years until fire triggers the growth of seedlings from the ashes.

Many small animals such as the mountain brushtail possum, have no choice but to try to sit out a bushfire, sheltering in hollows of large trees, in logs, or underground.

Bracken ferns have interconnected underground root systems that help them recover quickly from fire, and they often provide some of the first green life after a fire.

Gum trees put out new, green leafy stems called epicormic shoots from buds buried safely beneath the burnt bark.

Some trees such as the tall mountain ash depend on fire to trigger the release of seeds from their woody fruits. The seeds benefit from the nutrient-rich bed of ash and sunlight on the forest floor.

15

Listed: Yellowstone National Park, USA, the pyramids at Giza, Egypt, and the Galapagos Islands, Ecuador.

World heritage

Listing the world's natural and cultural treasures.

There are about 1000 places across the world inscribed on the World Heritage List, including temples and other buildings, islands, caves, national parks, relics, works of art and waterways, in countries from Afghanistan to Zimbabwe. The list, kept by the United Nations, was started in 1978 with just 12 items, but more are added each year. Australia now has 19 wonders on the list (see pages 18–19).

The aim of the list is to protect places of outstanding cultural and natural value for the whole world. There are 10 reasons to put something on the list – six cultural reasons and four natural – and many places fulfil several criteria. For example, Kakadu National Park is listed for both its cultural and natural heritage values.

The first World Heritage List, in 1978, included such diverse places as the Galapagos Islands in Ecuador, Aachen Cathedral in Germany, the Wieliczka Salt Mine in Poland and Yellowstone National Park in the USA.

WHL Criteria

What do you need to be to become World Heritage listed?

1. A masterpiece of human creative genius.
2. Something that exhibits an important interchange of human values, over a span of time or within a cultural area.
3. An exceptional representation of a cultural tradition or civilisation.
4. An outstanding example of building, structure or landscape that illustrates a significant stage in human history.
5. An outstanding example of a traditional human settlement, land-use, or sea-use that is representative of a culture.
6. Something associated with events, living traditions, ideas or beliefs of outstanding universal significance.
7. An area of exceptional natural beauty.
8. Outstanding examples of major stages in earth's history, including the record of life or geological processes.
9. Outstanding examples representing significant on-going ecological and biological processes in the evolution and development of ecosystems.
10. The most important natural habitats for conservation of biodiversity.

Listed: The world's third largest hot spring at Yellowstone National Park, USA, and the ruins of Machu Picchu, Peru.

PHOTOGRAPHS BY: NICK RAINS

Our World Herit

Our places that have made the list.

In 1981, just three years after the World Heritage List was first created, Australia had three sites listed: The Great Barrier Reef, Kakadu National Park and the Willandra Lakes Region, NSW, home to Australia's oldest human remains. Australia now has 19 wonders listed, from the remote sub-Antarctic islands — Heard, McDonald and Macquarie — to the Sydney Opera House and the Royal Exhibition Building and Carlton Gardens in Melbourne. Some of the listings, such as the Gondwana Rainforests and the Tasmanian Wilderness, take in several national parks. The most recent Australian listing, in 2010, was the Australian Convict Sites, which are 11 locations across the country steeped in our convict history.

Listed: Purnululu National Park (above) and the Gondwana Rainforests of Queensland (right).

KAKADU NATIONAL
WORLD HERITAGE

NORTHERN
TERRITORY

PURNULULU NATIONAL PARK
WORLD HERITAGE AREA

NINGALOO COAST
WORLD HERITAGE AREA

WESTERN
AUSTRALIA

ULURU-KATA TJUTA NATIONAL
PARK WORLD HERITAGE ARE

SHARK BAY, WESTERN AUSTRALIA
WORLD HERITAGE AREA

Australian Convict Sites ¤

3980 km

Heard Island and
McDonald Islands MRR

HEARD AND
McDONALD
ISLANDS
WHA

¤ World Heritage Site
World Heritage Area
National Park
Indigenous Protected Area
Other protected area
Marine protected area

0   250   500 km

AG CARTOGRAPHIC DIVISION
DATA: COMMONWEALTH OF AUSTRALIA, SEWPaC

age areas

AG CARTOGRAPHIC DIVISION
DATA: COMMONWEALTH OF AUSTRALIA, SEWPaC

FAST FACT
In Purnululu National Park is the Bungle Bungle Range, which is made of quartz sandstone that has eroded over 20 million years into a series of amazing beehive-shaped towers or cones.

The Great Barrier Reef, listed in 1981, was one of Australia's first areas to receive World Heritage status.

WET TROPICS OF QUEENSLAND
WORLD HERITAGE AREA

STRALIAN FOSSIL MAMMAL SITES (RIVERSLEIGH / NARACOORTE) WORLD HERITAGE AREA

GREAT BARRIER REEF
WORLD HERITAGE AREA

QUEENSLAND

FRASER ISLAND
WORLD HERITAGE AR

SOUTH
USTRALIA

NEW SOUTH

GONDWANA RAINFORESTS OF
AUSTRALIA WORLD HERITAGE AREA

WILLANDRA LAKES REGION
WORLD HERITAGE AREA

LORD HOWE ISLAND GROUP
WORLD HERITAGE AREA

WALES

GREATER BLUE MOUNTAINS
AREA WORLD HERITAGE AREA

¤ Sydney Opera House
Australian Convict Sites

ACT

VICTORIA

¤ Royal Exhibition Building
and Carlton Gardens

1400 km

Norfolk
Island NP   *Norfolk Island*
        Norfolk
        Island BG
            Nepean I
Norfolk
Island NP
        Phillip I

TASMANIA   ¤ Australian Convict Sites

TASMANIAN WILDERNESS
WORLD HERITAGE AREA

¤ Australian Convict Sites

1550 km

MACQUARIE   *Macquarie*
ISLAND WHA   *Island*
                Macquarie
                Island CMR
Macquarie
Island MP

CLOCKWISE FROM TOP LEFT: JASON EDWARDS (JE), JE, JE, ESTHER BEATON, ROD SCOTT, JOHN PICKRELL, JE

Tasmania's finest

The magic of Cradle Mountain-Lake St Clair National Park.

Tasmania has 19 great national parks, and Cradle Mountain-Lake St Clair National Park, in the centre of the island state, is one of the best loved.

In the park you'll see dramatic snow-covered mountains in winter, alpine tarns surrounded by ancient, gnarled pine trees, button-grass meadows, and dark and wild forests. It is home to Tasmanian devils, wombats, Bennetts wallabies and quolls.

A very special plant, called the deciduous beech, fagus or tanglefoot, is found around the popular Dove Lake and Crater Lake area. More of a low-growing, tangled shrub than a tree, it grows to about 2m high and has tiny green leaves, as small as your fingernails, that turn sunset colours of gold, orange and red during April and May. It is special because it is the only Australian native plant that loses its leaves over winter. It is only found in cold areas of Tasmania, usually above an altitude of 800m in areas with a fairly high rainfall. Scientists recently discovered that one deciduous beech tree is 350 years old.

One of the most famous long-distance bushwalks in the country, called the Overland Track, cuts through Cradle Mountain-Lake St Clair National Park. Each year, about 8000 people hike this 80km track over five or six days, either carrying their tents, food and all equipment in big backpacks, or paying extra to stay in huts with hot water where meals are cooked for them.

Fun year-round, summer's the best time for wildlife spotting, but in winter the deciduous beeches turn yellow.

Boardwalk sections of the Overland Track are repaired yearly after about 8000 pairs of feet tread them.

Indigenous Protected Areas

Where culture and conservation meet.

Indigenous Protected Areas account for nearly a quarter of Australia's National Reserve System. They are areas of land or sea whose traditional owners – Aboriginals or Torres Strait Islanders – have entered into an agreement with the Australian Government to improve and protect biodiversity, while conserving traditional culture.

The areas are managed to maintain culture, provide employment for indigenous people, develop skills and find income sources for traditional owners to look after their country. Indigenous people might be employed in the areas as rangers, tour guides or bush-food suppliers.

The first Indigenous Protected Area was declared in 1998, and there are now 51 such areas across the country, encompassing more than 365,000sq.km.

The smallest is Pulu Islet in the Torres Strait, at just 15ha, and the largest is the Tanami Indigenous Protected Area in the Northern Territory, covering 101,500sq.km.

In Victoria, the Lake Condah Indigenous Protected Area helps protect endangered species such as the common bent-wing bat, heath mouse and growling grass frog. It also holds a remarkable, ancient piece of engineering dating back 6600 years: a system of pools, weirs and ponds in which the Gunditjmara Aboriginal people raised and trapped fish and eels as part of a fully functioning system of fish farming. It is one of the world's oldest constructions. In recent times, four generations of Gunditjmara people have helped rebuild one of the weirs.

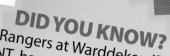

Because of their isolation the Fraser Island dingoes are the purest strain of dingo in eastern Australia.

It is estimated that there are 130-200 dingoes that call Fraser Island their home.

Our island

If you go to Great Sandy National Park, on Fraser Island off the coast of Queensland, you will almost certainly see a dingo or two, trotting along the beach, or creeping around a campsite. They are clever and crafty, and will often take any food left lying around.

There are estimated to be about 200 dingoes on the island. They are a native, wild dog, and the dingoes on Fraser Island are some of the purest in Australia, because they haven't mixed with domestic dogs very much.

Rangers in our national parks often have to deal with tricky issues and make difficult decisions, and that is certainly the case on Fraser Island.

Because some visitors have illegally fed the dingoes and encouraged them to come close for photographs, a few dingoes have become very used to people, and even aggressive, sometimes

dingoes

nipping at or biting people. In 2001, a nine-year-old boy was killed by dingoes on Fraser Island.

As a result, the rangers spend a lot of time talking to campers about dingoes and correct behaviour around them. Some of the campsites have special fences to keep out dingoes.

Rangers have put special satellite collars on dingoes in order to study their movements and understand their behaviour better. But each year the rangers kill a handful of dingoes that they believe have become too dangerous.

Some people think that the dingoes are not dangerous and rangers should not kill them or stop people feeding them. Other people want the rangers to do more to make Fraser Island safer for people.

What would you do if you were a ranger on Fraser Island?

DID YOU KNOW?
Aboriginals on Fraser Island call dingoes "wongaree" or "wongadee". Traditionally they used them as camp dogs.

Protecting the seas

Our network of marine reserves.

Australia is developing the largest network of marine reserves in the world, protecting reefs, islands, sandy beaches, vast seagrass meadows, mangroves and underwater canyons.

Our oldest, biggest and most famous marine park is the 348,000sq.km Great Barrier Reef Marine Park, established in 1975. It protects some 1500 types of fish and 400 coral species in the world's largest and healthiest collection of coral reefs.

But there are more than 200 other marine protected areas, controlled by state, territory and federal governments, which aim to conserve our rich sea life and the underwater habitats in which they live.

The Waterfall-Fortescue Marine Conservation Area off the east coast of Tasmania protects an underwater forest! The forest is made of giant kelp, which is a type of seaweed that can grow up to 50cm a day, up to 30m tall, forming dense canopies above the sea floor that provide important fish-breeding areas. Such areas are considered to be the marine environment's most diverse and productive habitats, but up to 95% of Australia's giant kelp forests have been destroyed.

Marine parks are generally managed for different uses, so fishing is allowed in some areas and big container ships use other areas. Studies have shown that fish in marine sanctuaries where fishing is not allowed tend to grow bigger and carry more eggs, helping to restock the surrounding areas.

Clownfish are sensitive to changes in water temperature, which can destroy their food source.

DID YOU KNOW?
Great Barrier Reef, is the largest reef system in the world, but it is not continuous. It consists of about 3000 broken-up individual reefs, of which 760 are fringing reefs along the mainland or around islands.

ESTHER BEATON

The red of Kata Tjuṯa and Uluṟu is actually a thin layer of iron oxcide that coats mostly grey rock.

Let's rock!

Two of our rock stars are found in the Red Centre.

Uluṟu-Kata Tjuṯa National Park is best known for the massive, hulking rock called Uluru, which changes colour into reds, pinks, oranges and purple at sunrise and sunset everyday.

Uluṟu is actually the top of a seam of sandstone that probably continues underground for several kilometres. We see the above ground part of it because the landscape around the sandstone has been eroded away. Its summit is 348m above the surrounding plain.

Uluṟu was originally the name of a waterhole high on The Rock. You pronounce the word by using vowel sounds like in the word "pull". It was named Ayers Rock by its first non-Aboriginal visitors in 1873.

The other large features in the 1325sq.km national park are a collection of 36 huge rounded sandstone domes called Kata Tjuṯa, or The Olgas.

Found in the middle of Australia, this World Heritage Area is recognised for both its natural and cultural values. Tourists have been coming here since 1936. The park is owned by the Aṉangu Aboriginal people, but managed by a federal government body, Environment Australia.

ESTHER BEATON

DID YOU KNOW?
For many years, the Anangu people have asked that visitors not climb the track up Uluṟu. A better alternative is the 10km walk around the base, which has signs explaining much of the Aboriginal stories about the rock.

Meet a ranger

We interview **Max Orchard**, a ranger on Christmas Island in the Indian Ocean.

Where is Christmas Island?
"Christmas Island is way out in the Indian Ocean, 1540km west of the Australian mainland. It is much closer to Singapore, and is only 360km south of Jakarta, the capital of Indonesia. About 1800 people live here."

SORREL WILBY

Do you have any favourite species?
"The frigatebirds are just amazing birds. There are three species here: the greater frigatebird, the lesser frigatebird and the Christmas Island frigatebird. Every one of them has a different personality – just like people," says Max. "The robber crabs are also interesting characters."

Do you need to help the wildlife?
"In my spare time, my wife Beverley and I have cared for a lot of injured and orphaned seabirds that otherwise wouldn't have survived."

What species does the national park there protect?
"The national park covers about 63% of Christmas Island, and there are more endemic species [animals found nowhere else] here than any other park in Australia: Abbotts booby, Christmas Island frigatebird, the Christmas Island hawk-owl, to name a few. Of course, its most famous residents are the 50 million red crabs that migrate across the island each year and the world's largest population of robber crabs."

Glossary

Algae A type of plant

Antifreeze A liquid used to stop freezing

Biologist A person who studies living things

Breed To produce young

Canine teeth Big, sharp teeth on each side of the jaw

Colonies Groups of plants or animals of the same kind living together

Echolocation A method used by some animals to 'see' objects by sending out sounds and detecting echoes that bounce back

Ecosystem An interconnected web of the animals, plants, soil, weather and other elements in an area

Extinct When no members of a species are alive

Fungus A plant-like organism related to mushroooms and moulds

Incubating Hatching eggs by keeping them warm

Invertebrate A small animal without a backbone

Lichen A type of plant created by fungi and algae living closely together

Mammal A type of warm-blooded animal with fur that feeds its young milk

Pack ice Ice floating on the sea that has been driven together into large blocks by winds or ocean currents

Plankton Very tiny plants or animals living in seawater

Sea ice Ice that forms in autumn and winter on top of the ocean once the surface temperature drops to freezing point

Species Types of plants or animals that are alike and have the same features

World Heritage Areas assessed by the United Nations as deserving protection

Further reading & internet sites

Christmas Island:
VIDEO: www.australiangeographic.com.au/journal/christmas-and-cocos-islands.htm
www.environment.gov.au/parks/christmas

Dingoes on Fraser Island:
VIDEO: www.australiangeographic.com.au/journal/video-fraser-island-dingoes.htm

Gilbert's potoroo:
www.australiangeographic.com.au/journal/back-from-the-dead-gilberts-potoroo.htm
www.potoroo.org

Kakadu National Park:
www.australiangeographic.com.au/journal/kakadu-the-land-of-wet-and-dry.htm
www.australiangeographic.com.au/journal/view-image.htm?index=0&gid=9346

World Heritage
www.australiangeographic.com.au/journal/australias-world-heritage-sites.htm
http://whc.unesco.org/en/list/
www.environment.gov.au/heritage/places/world/list.html

Uluṟu-Kata Tjuṯa
www.australiangeographic.com.au/journal/uluru-handing-the-rock-back.htm
www.australiangeographic.com.au/journal/view-image.htm?index=0&gid=7497

Index

Aboriginals 6, 12–13, 22–23, 25, 28–29

Bioregion..4

Ecosystem 4

Endangered animals 6, 19, 22–23

Feral animals 10, 12–13

Fire....................................12–13, 14–15

Fraser Island 18–19, 24–25

Great Barrier Reef.........18–19, 26–27

Habitat.......................... 8, 12–13, 26–27

**Kakadu
National Park** 6–7, 16–17, 18–19

**Ngaanyatjarra Lands Indigenous
Protected Area** 4, 22–23

Pollution 26–27

Rock art 6, 12–13

**Uluru-Kata Tjuṯa
National Park** ....18 –19, 28–29

Last shot

Big western grey kangaroos are found across southern Australia from just south of Shark Bay, WA, inland along the Murray—Darling Basin through to southern Queensland. This fortunate roo has found his way to Lucky Bay in Cape Le Grand National Park, Esperance, WA.

Australian GEOGRAPHIC EDUCATION

Editor
Ken Eastwood

Sub-editor
Natsumi Penberthy

Designer
Filip Bartkowiak

Picture research
Jess Teideman

Prepress
Filip Bartkowiak

Editor-in-chief
Ian Connellan

SUBSCRIPTIONS

Group circulation manager
Paul Weaving

Brand manager
Nevenka Moulakas

Email: magshop@magshop.com.au
Phone: 136 116

Send us letters:
Australian Geographic Education
GPO Box 4088
Sydney NSW 2001

Or email us:
education@australiangeographic.
com.au

MEDIA GROUP

Managing director
Matthew Stanton

Publishing director
Gerry Reynolds

Publisher, Specialist Division
Brendon Hill

Associate Publisher, Specialist Division
Jo Runciman

Other titles in this series:

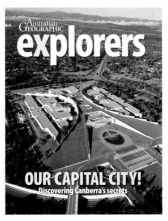